MORE PICTURES TO GROW UP WITH

EDITED BY BRYAN HOLME

MORE
PICTURES
TO GROW UP WITH

By

Katharine Gibson

AMERICAN STUDIO BOOKS

NEW YORK AND LONDON

What the Book Contains

Pictures in Color

Who Painted the Pictures

Introduction

A MODERN British writer, Aldous Huxley, speaks of picture frames as "doorways to other worlds." These other worlds contain much that is not in this everyday world—princesses and clowns, shepherds and angels, peasants of long ago dancing, fashionable, bustled ladies walking sedately under small parasols. To look at any book of pictures is to travel as widely as the mood suits you. Like a magician holding the secret of all calendars, you can go back and forth in time from the days of the knights in the Italian hill town of Sienna to Paris, its painters, and to tomorrow.

It is not just the outside world you see through the doorway of picture frames, but the artist's own separate, private world. Three friends were talking about apples at luncheon the other day. The first one said she hated apples and always had and she knew why. Her earliest memory of an apple was also a memory of herself when she was too young to understand much of anything. A bad little boy, five years old or so, gave her a green apple and told her it was good. See, he was eating his, every bit! She could not guess that his was ripe and, not to be outdone, bravely ate her own down to the core. No, she had never liked apples.

The second friend said she loved apples and always would. Her father, whom she especially worshipped, was a busy man and she saw all too little of him. But when fall came, no matter how pressing his concerns, he always hitched up the old brown family horse and took her out to the farm on some Saturday afternoon. He took just her and no one else, for it was their special expedition. He never failed. Her importance in his eyes and the sparkle of frost in the air, made the apples they picked something not quite of this earth. Yes, she had always liked apples.

The third friend said she was of two minds about apples. When she was so little that she had not yet discovered that "this is mine" and "that is yours," she walked quite innocently into a neighbor's yard and picked an apron full of apples from under the trees. A lean, cross old woman screamed at her and so frightened her that she ran tumbling home without as much as a leaf left in her apron. No one had ever spoken to her like that. Why it had happened she did not know. Sitting beside her on the back steps, her mother pealed and quartered an apple for her, taken from a basket in the kitchen. As the pealings curled from the knife, her mother explained quietly the difference between your own yard and someone elses. The pieces of apple were received somewhat gingerly. They were sweet enough, but had in them the uncertain flavor of fright and the remembered bitterness of the old woman's voice. That friend wasn't sure—she never had been—whether she liked apples or not.

Suppose those three people had painted apples, the same apples. The first apples, no matter what their actual color, would probably have been a stomach-ache green against a mustard yellow background. The second apples would have been round, a shining deep red, making you think of fall leaves and bonfires and cold cider. How the third, who was of two minds about apples, would have painted them is difficult to guess. Perhaps some would have been ripe and inviting like the one her mother gave her, and the others green and hard as an unjust word. But certainly those three pictures, had they been painted, would not have been the same.

One of the most fascinating things about looking at pictures is to try to figure out how the artist felt about what was before him, also, how he actually saw it. A giant pine is nearby. Would the artist think the great solid trunk could best be painted with a heavy pull of the brush while the delicate needles with the sun and shadows playing through them needed only thinly etched lines, or would he think of it in terms of the dark and light pattern of branch against branch, with the pale sky in between? Look through this book just at trees, then just at faces, then at flowers and at skies. It is the artists that are different, not the apples or the pines or the other things they painted.

After you have patiently looked at all these, you will probably find some you don't like at all. You certainly wouldn't have chosen to paint that picture, or, if you had, you would have done it very differently—which is quite all right! Unfortunately, most of us were brought up with the idea that we should like art. Almost certainly at some time, someone has said, "There is a great picture; you ought to like it. Everybody does." Now what you like or don't like is strictly your own affair. No one has the right to tell you what to like. No artist can paint a picture with the purpose of asking you to like it, though he may hope you will understand it.

Try to find out, if you can, a little of what the artist saw; try to feel and to understand what he felt. The more of these new worlds, seen through the open doorways of picture frames, that you understand, the more you may begin to like them. To like a thing is, after all, just to feel at home with it.

Animals and Birds

To KNOW an animal well enough to draw him at all completely is a very lengthy undertaking. To know, say a rabbit, is not merely to be able to recognize him by his long ears and cotton tail as he runs. It is being able to see beneath his fur to bone and muscle; it is knowing, for instance, how his long hind legs and his shorter front ones are built and it is remembering how he moves when he runs, what happens when he sits up or down, hops or bounds. Also, it is a matter of becoming acquainted with him for what he is as you would with a human being. For instance, there is his timidity, his gentleness, his swiftness, his particular enjoyment of long naps, his good appetite for carrots and garden lettuce. Then his little personal habits are to be watched, the way he wrinkles his nose, or thumps with his hind foot when he's angry. This may seem like a long way around to come up to the simple drawing of a rabbit. But a really great animal drawing is born of such knowledge and understanding.

The artist must *feel* with the animal as though he had lived beside him in his small house; he must learn how the little creature's heart jumps when a fox barks above him or how he grows giddy for joy when he plays with his fellows in a remote field at twilight, as most assuredly he does. This is the kind of knowing that went into Albrecht Dürer's drawing of a "Hare" which you will find on one of the next pages.

Certainly it is not suggested that you wait until you know all this before you begin to draw your first bunny. The other side of the story is that the more you draw an animal, the more you learn about it. You have looked at your dog a thousand times, but if you want to realize how little you have seen, ask yourself, when he's not around to show you, what exactly he does do with his hind legs when he sits down.

Moreover, many fascinating drawings have been made that do not give a complete picture of an animal and were never intended to. Such a drawing sets out not to tell a whole story, but just to say one thing about a creature. That is what Sesshū has done with his Gibbon monkey. And yet to make a passing glimpse seem so exactly right, it was necessary for Sesshū to be very sure of what the things were about a monkey that made him look most like a monkey. Often an artist thinks of an animal chiefly as a decoration, as did the Persian painter of the chained lion. Sometimes, too, the animal becomes a motive in a design, like the rabbit in the Coptic textile.

Whatever the intention of the artist, there is always the added question of his tools—how shall he use them and which ones? A tortoise shell angora kitten lies half asleep on a favorite chair in the clear New Hampshire sunshine. His dark and light spots at once suggest the use of a pencil; his flat patches of orange, yellow, black, suggest a crayon and his long graceful curves, the clean lines of a pen. But that lightning movement of a paw as a fly buzzes past could just be caught, perhaps, by the most rapid stroke of a wet brush. The sheen of sunlight, the soft feel of the kitten's coat could best be given by oil paints, rich and thick to show contrast, or to blend as they do in Juan Mazo's painting of Maria Teresa's silky spaniel. Certainly no one can work in all these ways on one drawing or painting at one time. What's to decide it? Only the artist knows. But in looking at these pictures, see how near you can come to figuring out for yourself something of the secret of his choice.

Opposite: *Poets have written volumes about beauty and how it cannot be dimmed or destroyed by time: "Its loveliness increases; it will never pass into nothingness." An unknown Greek sculptor modeled this* HORSE *more than twenty-three hundred years ago—perfectly formed, gay, light-stepping as the wind, he moves through time.*

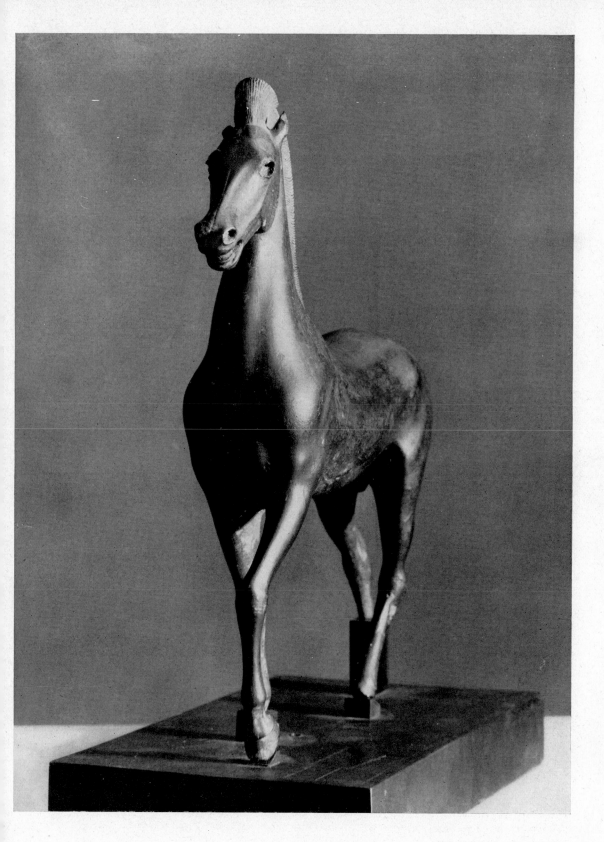

When first looked at, this picture, made by an Indian painter back in the 17th Century, USTAD MANSUR, seems chiefly remarkable for its pattern. But look again and notice how the drawing is filled with the secret life of the little striped "not-quite" horse. See how he stands, ready to move at a whisper, eye wide open, ears pricked up. Here is a living design. But that is what a *Zebra* is! Many artists have drawn the stripes; few, the breathing creature himself.

Alert, the beautifully patterned duck watches while his mate sleeps lightly and comfortably on the soft featherbed that is herself. The unknown 17th Century Indian painter has caught perfectly a moment in the life of these *Two Ducks*. He has also managed to dip his brush deep in the main current of bird-life—migrating, meeting, nesting—unchanging in all times and places. He painted not just those two ducks that he saw so long ago, but all ducks that have ever lived.

19

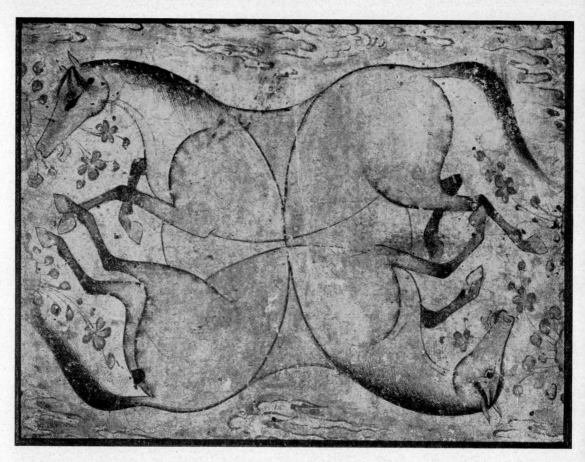

How many horses can you see? Two? Turn the book the other way up. Two more! The clever design of *Four Horses,* built out of circles, was drawn by a Persian artist some three hundred years ago. Study it. It will tell you a good deal about some of the important shapes in a horse's body; it will show you much about lines, how they may be clearly made, how accented lightly, how strengthened with a dark and shadowed touch. Notice the little flowers in the background, rarely lacking in some shape or form in a Persian out-of-door painting. Now make a puzzle-design like this, yourself, using your cat or dog instead of a horse.

Opposite: From the tip of his delicate fur-edged ear to his long, useful scratching claws, all that makes this creature what he is and unlike every other, was put down once and for all by the great German artist, ALBRECHT DÜRER in the year 1502. Notice the thickness and pattern of the fur, the springing whiskers of this *Hare*.

Albertina Museum, Vienna

EDWARD HICKS, an early American painter, largely untrained, but with an alert eye and vigorous brush, has painted *The Peaceable Kingdom,* where the "lion lies down with the lamb." It must be said that the lion, and especially the leopard, seem unpleasantly astonished to find their fierce dispositions so unaccountably changed. In the distance, William Penn is signing his peace treaty with the Indians.

With luscious, thick strokes of his brush and rich colors, one sparkling into the other, the Spanish artist, MAZO, has painted the fevered, restless pet of a princess who, by gently holding him down by his silky ear, keeps him prisoner on his too-soft cushion. This little picture is a detail from the painting *Infanta Maria Teresa*.

23

Angry, fearless, the royal *Cock,* by an unknown 17th Century Mughal painter, moves forward. He is spirited from dagger-sharp beak to quivering, fanned-out tail, every separate feather vibrating with life. With a drawing of this kind, it is easier to see a lot if you see only a little. Tear a hole in a piece of paper about the size of the cock's head. Move it over the picture slowly and look separately at comb, eye, beak, feathers, and claws. Watch the lines change, now strong and black, now light as an eyelash. When you have found your favorite spot, draw it so large it will cover your entire paper. Remember, then, that this was made not with a pencil, a crayon, or a pen, but with a brush, and think what control of hand was behind that brush.

This *Hare* by an unknown Persian artist of the 17th Century is not only more natural, but also more alive than the king of beasts, shown below. Even his whiskers are alert. This drawing and the one below set forth perfectly two very different ways of seeing animals.

The *Chained Lion* seems a bit dumbfounded at being held prisoner. He is thinking out the situation. Notice what attention has been given by the unknown 16th Century Persian artist to the detail of the chains. You cannot forget that the lion is captive.

Gerald Nailor, Navaho Indian artist, has made a pattern of long-legged horses, a little spotted colt, and two women, strong and quiet after the manner of his people. The artist has shown a delicate sense of design, both in the gradations from light to dark of the accordian-like folds of the riders' skirts and in the slender leaves and stems of the plants. He shows a feeling for clean, clear lines, as well as a respect for the white surface of his paper. The background has the same relation to the forms drawn upon it that silence has to sound. It is the bell that rings against the quietness of a country evening that echoes longest, not the tolling drowned in a thousand city sounds. So the shapes in *Navaho Women on Horses* gain by the blankness of background.

This small part of an ancient Egyptian wall painting, *Horses and Mules at the Harvest Field,* shows with carefulness, yet with what spirit, the artist (unknown) worked. The black horses are fiery and eager to be off.

British Museum

Below: These horses were painted by the artist, KLITIAS, on a narrow band around the neck of a *Greek Vase* made by the potter, ERGOTIMOS, more than twenty-four hundred years ago. The vase around which they run, is called the François vase after the name of the man who first discovered it. Because of its size, the perfection of its shape, the superb draughtsmanship of the artist, and also because of the stories it tells, this vase is one of the most famous works of art to come from the most gifted of nations. The chariot, driver and horses, are part of the funeral procession of the friend of great Achilles, Patroklus, a hero who fell before the walls of Troy.

Archeological Museum, Florence

A 16th Century Persian artist, probably SULTAN MUHAMMAD, has drawn this spirited *Camel With his Driver* in outline and with practically no shading. Rarely is an artist able to do so much just with line—to give such a sense of weight, of rapid motion, even of roundness. Quite aside from all they have to tell, these lines make a fine, clear, clean-edged design. Notice how the very dark spots point the drawing up and give it strength—the driver's buttons and mustache, the camel's tail, eye, harness and anklet bells.

Iranian Institute

Museum of Fine Arts, Boston

Everybody knows an *Elephant* is large, slow moving, and heavy. But it takes the keen eye of an Indian artist to see the wonderfully intricate patterns and closely harmonized grey tones of his loose raincoat skin. This fine beast was used, in the days when he was painted, to carry princes and Eastern potentates on their travels and hunting parties. Note the bell under his chin, the tame expression in his eyes. The artist is unknown but the painting is attributed to a Mughal artist of the 16th Century.

29

Combined in this painting of a *Kingfisher on Trunk of Tree,* by an unknown Indian painter of over two hundred years ago, is the accuracy of a scientist's work, the grace of a decoration and a deep, almost humorous understanding of the bird himself. For puzzled young ornithologists, it must be added, this is not the American kingfisher.

A very small part of the much larger painting *Monkeys and Birds in Trees,* but enough! With the fewest possible soft touches of his brush, the artist, Sesshū, has painted a mother gibbon monkey and baby who comfortably rides upon her head and shoulders. "But Sesshū made the arms too long!" According to inch by inch measurements, perhaps you are right. But this is not just a picture of a monkey—it's a picture of what you see when a monkey moves quickly past you, still but for an instant.

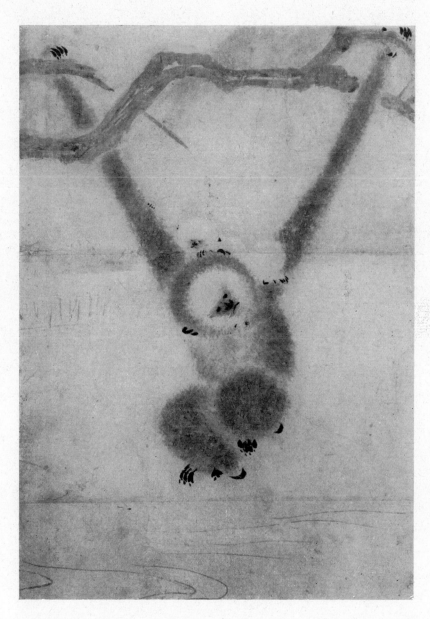

This *Rabbit,* on a Coptic textile, made from linen threads some two thousand years ago, is enough to make the saying "timid as a bunny" seem at least questionable. The whole pattern has a strength and vigor which is not unlike that of the greedy little beast. Notice how rabbit, grapes, leaves, stem are fitted together and into the woven square.

In ancient Egyptian wall paintings, there are other finer pictures of cats, but perhaps none so full of life as this *Cat Under a Chair*. Tied to the carved foot of a chair, her dish of food just out of reach, every hair of the creature bristles with bafflement and rage. This shows the clawing, mewing, scratching side of the animal. Purrs and contentment are as far away as the unreachable dinner. Here is a complete portrait of a word, and the word is "catty." Notice that the unknown Egyptian artist, who lived 1473-1448 B.C., was more than a little uncertain about where the tail belonged. He made two tries, neither quite correct.

Photograph: Cleveland Museum of Art

大熊貓是my
年偷款動路圖
二稿圖多兒號台
關心不覺嚴此至
幼寫出現示家後
覚其用情各不為
動作辨選僕怕喘
我可為音開真大
一九五九年
守劊

(From "Chin Pao and the Giant Pandas" by Chiang Yee, courtesy the publishers)

34

Above: This *Rooster* was carved out of wood by some unknown American ancestor who was "handy" with chisel and knife. It has a combination of liveliness and a feeling for pattern and design for which the trained artist often struggles in vain.

Opposite: Against a background of mountains, pale with Spring mist, the baby Giant Panda looks with peering, black-rimmed eyes out of a mask-like face, topped by soft, alerted ears. The Panda is the mighty clown of beasts, and like the clown of fable and stories, he seems sad beneath his costume of white with neat short black jacket and elegant black-gloved paws. *Mao-mao* is a character from the Chinese artist CHIANG YEE's enchanting book "Chin-Pao and the Giant Pandas."

Except in the art of the East, rarely is such observation and understanding of animals coupled with such beauty of design. Anyone who knows bears, knows that they talk. It is easy enough to understand that these *Three Bear Cubs*, by an unknown 15th Century Persian artist, are quarreling. Say the little bears on the ground—"Just because there's a bee in that tree, that's no sign there's honey. Come on down or you'll get stung on your poke-it-in-nose." Replies the cub in the tree—"Suppose you think you'll find honey in rocks! When I do get honey, who'll eat it? Not you two, Smarty-paws!"

36

These *Birds in an Acacia Tree* sang, nested, searched for food along the lotus-bordered Nile in Egypt nearly four thousand years ago. The secret life of a bird, to be guessed at now in the brightness of an eye, the flirt of a tail, or in the unfolding of a wing, was caught by the brush of this ancient Egyptian painter so perfectly that the birds seem alive now, this minute, as if it were spring in our own South. What a feeling of pattern the artist gives in the design of leaves and feathers, the balance of dark areas against light.

Photograph: Cleveland Museum of Art

It is a little hard to say why this engraving by MARTIN SCHONGAUER is so appealing. Perhaps it is because it has such quiet simplicity. None but a great artist could draw so clearly and surely; none but a great artist could combine two creatures in so perfect a design or set them down so well within their oblong space. Yet having done that much, Martin Schongauer was content to say, "Enough." Another reason why this small print of *Two Deer* is so delightful and so important is that the artist showed an almost childlike fondness and understanding of the antlered buck and grazing doe.

Opposite: This is a small part of a painting of *Saint Jerome* by the Italian artist, GIOVANNI BELLINI. The timidity and bravery of all wild creatures is in this meeting of two young rabbits, gravely watched over by a sentinel squirrel, and a keen-eyed hawk in the branches above. Trees, bridges, castle, and a distant city seem but temporary man-made things compared with the shy greeting of the two small creatures as Bellini has painted them. You will find this an excellent picture from which to draw. Notice how beautifully it is composed—put together—in its frame made by the rocky entrance to St. Jerome's cave.

The Artist Tells a Story

Throughout history, the artist has told in pictures the story of his time and country, what he believed and what he wanted to make-believe. Long ago, when very few people could read or write, stories could best be recorded in painting or sculpture, and those who could afford it employed artists to paint their favorite stories for them—on walls, on wood, on pottery or else to carve them in stone as great monuments.

Ancient Egyptian pharoahs wanted records in pictures and sculpture of their daily life on the Nile, examples of which we have found in tombs. The Greeks, too, wanted stories and, as well as writing them, they painted the adventures of their mythological heroes on vases or shaped their gods in carvings on their temples. In the Europe of the early Middle Ages, stories from the Bible were most often told in stained glass, in wool on their tapestries, in carved ivory, wood or stone, also in primitive paintings and in richly decorated parchment pages of the early books illuminated by monks. Then, during the fifteen and sixteen hundreds, the great Italian artists carried on the telling of Bible stories, but not so much for the sake of the story as for the joy of making great, majestic compositions in the new technique of oil painting on canvas. As did all the world at this time, they looked back to what seemed to them the golden days of Greece and Rome and thought to make those days live again. This was the rebirth or *Renaissance* and it is by this name that the time in which they lived is known. They, too, painted the heroes Odysseus, Herakles, Theseus, and the nymphs and fauns. During this time, the art of printing was also being perfected and more and more books appeared. Stories began to be read, not just looked at as they had been before. Gradually, then, artists turned to painting the outdoors, portraits, and pleasant scenes of family life.

In our time, artists have made many experiments with new combinations of line and shape, new kinds of design, and new ways of putting on color. More and more they have gone inside themselves and painted their own ideals and dreams. Today, storytelling in pictures is found here and there on the inside walls of a few buildings, but mostly so high up that no one can see them.

It is hard to know what is the most charming part of this painting by the Italian artist, Bernardo Martorell. Is it the slender lance-like figure of the knight in his pointed Gothic armor, the princess with her jeweled butterfly headdress, the castle, crowded by anxious watchers, or (if you like being safely frightened) is it the crouching, dog-like dragon? But who, after all, would not choose the horse, one of the loveliest creatures ever painted for any Saint George and the Dragon.

(Art Institute of Chicago)

For a very long time after people had learned to read and write, the printed page was the chief way in which people came to know stories. But perhaps now they have grown tired of just reading. "Tell me a story," is one of the first cries of a little child. The old man sits by the fire; he delights in relating the adventures of his youth. One of the deepest wants of mankind is still as persistent as it ever was. It may well be that this "want" again awaits the serious artist who can tell the old tales in a way that fits our times and yet is truly great and not just a repetition of the old stories. Heroism, such as the world has seldom known has been shown in recent times: perils will continue to be endured by unsung heroes through all time. But the story that will live as long as men have ears to hear with or eyes to see with must always be passed through the mind of a great storyteller or painted by a great artist. This is what we may be waiting for—now.

When that artist comes, he will be new but, however he works, he must build on the traditions of the old. He will look at the pictures storytellers make today and at the pictures of long ago—just the kinds of pictures you will see if you turn the next few pages of this book.

This painting of Saint George, so different from the one on page 40, was made on a wooden panel by an unknown Russian artist in the early fourteen hundreds. Its strong colors and flat, golden background were meant to be seen by the light of many candles on an altar. The worshipper thought of the young knight as the hero who could slay the vile beast by the power of his saintliness, rather than by a mere feat of strength.

43

From the figures at the right to the lifted golden trumpets at the left, this procession moves in a rising crescent of delight. As a perfume is compounded from the fragrance of many gardens, so this small miniature contains the very spirit of all the Maytime pilgrimages in the days of knights and silken ladies. It is one of a series of miniatures made by Pol de Limbourg and Jean Colombe for *The Book of Hours of the Duke of Berry,* far back in the fifteenth century.

Opposite: This is a detail from the *Unicorn Tapestry* series made in the time of Columbus. Woven from woolen threads, by the most skillful weavers of their day, they were a royal gift to Anne of Brittany, twice Queen of France. In the tapestries is told the story of the hunt for the unicorn who, more swift and brave than any other animal, could be captured only by a maiden. This detail from the seventh tapestry shows the unicorn fenced in, wearing a jeweled collar and fastened by a golden chain to a pomegranate tree. Never was a captive less truly captured. Head up, ears pricked for listening, plumed tail flicking, the unicorn will soon be away to the secret places where he lives.

This ancient Egyptian wall painting, by an unknown artist, tells the story of a morning in the *Harvest* fields. With difficulty, a servant holds the spirited horses of his master. Scribes keep track of the measures of grain as slaves gather it up. Below, the owner sits in a shaded bower while his servant stands beside him. Under the watchful eye of yet another scribe, more slaves bend rhythmically to cut the wheat with their curved sickles. In strips, copied by the modern "funnies," scene after scene is shown. Time has added little to the storytelling art of the painter since this was made. It shows just how it was one burning day on the Nile some three thousand years ago.

Opposite: This painting was done in the bottom of a *Greek Drinking Cup* or "kylix" by the artist, EUPHRONIOS, some twenty-four hundred years ago. With great delicacy, grace and strength, it tells how the hero, Theseus, proved to King Minos of Crete that he, Theseus, was in truth the son of Poseidon, God of the Sea. Theseus jumped into the ocean and, in the presence of the great Athena, was graciously received by Poseidon's queen, Amphitrite, who gave him a rich robe and a wondrous garland. These were her wedding gifts from the Goddess of Beauty, Aphrodite. Theseus, glittering with these treasures, rose from the water to the wonder of Minos and his court, who then knew him to be, beyond all doubting, the heir of great Poseidon.

46

Louvre, Paris

47

The Italian painter, GIOVANNI BELLINI, tells of the vision of Saint Francis of Assisi. Saint Francis stands before the rocks that have blossomed to make his home. If you would like to know this picture of *Saint Francis in Ecstasy* more fully, look at it with your pencil. It is a wonderful picture from which to draw. You will find that by enlarging the smaller objects, you can discover many complete pictures—the town, the listening donkey, a pattern of worn stones, or delicate plants. Little by little you will begin to feel that something of the serene beauty which Bellini made belongs to you.

Opposite: In pictures of *The Nativity,* Saint Joseph is often only a figure overshadowed by heavenly visitors and shepherds of kings. PETRUS CHRISTUS here has placed him in the foreground. He looks down, confident that he can care for the Child given into his keeping. Behind him are two delightful homespun angels astonished by their own stiffly soaring wings, gazing thoughtfully at the Child.

49

Here comes the Spring Bride! Village children, dogs, chickens and even a pig, all gather to see her. Seldom has a story of any event been told with more amusing completeness than in this picture of *The Whitsun-Bride* by PIETER BRUEGHEL, THE YOUNGER. Nothing is left out that could make the celebration more real; it is so real that it seems to go right on happening as you look, though some three hundred years have passed since the artist took part in it. The stir and excitement is even carried by hastening figures into the quiet outskirts of the village and beyond.

In this drawing, the English artist, ROWLANDSON, shows the Devonshire *Country Farm* of some two hundred years ago—nursery, laundry, pig pen, chicken yard noisily, cheerfully mixed. His clever, curving lines bring to life with equal skill the plump, bulging, sagging shapes of heavily thatched roof, round pigs, rounder children, full-skirted woman, squat little man and fat grain bags. Even the fence tells its story of hard persistent use that has softened every edge and corner.

Because he did not have the faith to believe the prophecy of an angel of the Lord concerning the miraculous birth of his son, who was to become the Baptist, Zacharias was struck dumb. When the prophecy was fulfilled, the child born, and the time for naming him came, Zacharias, unable to say the word, wrote his son's name upon a tablet. At that moment "his tongue was loosed and he spake blessing God." The Italian painter, called by the monks of his order, "Brother Angel" or FRA ANGELICO, tells this story of *The Naming of Saint John* as simply as though it had happened in some peaceful garden that he knew.

GERARD DAVID, the Flemish artist, with the carefully painted basket of swaddling bands, bundle of straw, welcoming nearness of the ox and the ass, has given a sense of how all that is humble was glorified by the Child who, laid in a manger, was worshipped first by poor shepherds. Notice with what wonderful delicacy in this *Nativity* the strong reds, blues, violets in the robes of Mary and Joseph are echoed with paler shades in the outstretched angels' wings.

The word "shepherd" has always stood for steadfastness and guarding care. "The Lord is my shepherd; I shall not want." Particularly in the days when men's livelihood came chiefly from the fields and beasts of the field, a shepherd who deserted his flock was considered the lowest of cowards. PIETER BRUEGHEL, THE ELDER, has made the point of his story of the *Unfaithful Shepherd,* who runs away and leaves his sheep to be devoured by a single wolf, even sharper by painting him so big and strong.

54

The Polish Rider by Rembrandt does not tell just one story, but many. It is the story of the romance, the loneliness, the danger of every soldier's venture into war. Ruin lies about him, strain and weariness are in his face and in the tense muscles of the horse. But freely, gallantly, he goes on, even though the falling darkness through which he must pass may be the darkness of death.

The aged Simeon received the Infant Jesus in the temple, saying, "Now lettest thy servant depart, O Lord, According to thy word in peace. For mine eyes have seen thy salvation." *The Presentation in the Temple* was painted in a golden moment of Italian art. The central figures keep their early simplicity and truthfulness to the spirit of the Bible story. At the same time, the artist, GIOVANNI DI PAOLO, brings into the painting not only the richness of costume and beauty of architecture of his own time, but also a new technical skill in painting more than just a flat background.

Opposite: Fascinated by the full-grown power (which painters had then just achieved) to push back walls and paint retreating colonnades and arches marching beneath arches, FRA CARNEVALE chose to tell more than one story in *The Birth of the Virgin*. He was able to create a separate setting for each individual story within the framework of one large composition. Try drawing the arches and circles, then the straight lines of walls and columns. You will soon feel how the parts of this painting interlock like the supporting stones in the span of a bridge.

(Both pictures courtesy The Metropolitan Museum of Art)

In this 14th century Persian version by RASHID AD-DIN, of the famous story of *Jonah and the Whale,* it would seem that all practical matters were thought of beforehand. Even before Jonah reaches the mainland, a heavenly being hastens to bring him a much needed shirt.

Opposite: By an unknown artist in India, this painting of *Noah's Ark,* with its well-ordered and graceful design, is certainly most complete in the way it explains the complex living arrangements about which most people have always wondered. Camels, elephants and all the heavy animals on the lowest deck; tigers, lions, leopards, monkeys, on the next; Noah and his family on top, and, appropriately, birds in the small "crow's-nest." The ark itself is completely fascinating, shaped like the dragons that lash about in the deep. Also not to be overlooked are the small cat on a ledge of the stern with his paws in his pockets quietly surveying the scene and the sailor, high in the rigging, poised like a ballet dancer.

(Mrs. Kirkor Minassian Collection)

The artist of the Middle Ages told Bible and other stories as though they had happened in the artist's own city and in the period when he lived. He did not bother with any time or place except his own. So *The Journey of the Magi* by SASSETTA is really the pilgrimage of some medieval duke or prince and his court, complete with jester, slim greyhounds, and even a monkey seated on the brocaded panniers of a donkey. Few pictures express more exquisitely the spirit of their own age, the early fifteen hundreds, than does this small, jewel-like detail.

Opposite: GIOVANNI DI PAOLO, an early Italian artist, paints the young Saint John as though he were a fair, angelic messenger. The slender figure leaves the safely walled city and goes alone to where the zig-zig pattern of planted fields gives way to sharp mountain peaks. Here is the story not only of John the Baptist, but also of any man who, "waxing strong in spirit," goes to prepare the way for unbelieving mankind. Half shut your eyes and look at *The Young Baptist Goes into the Wilderness* for the matchless beauty of the painting's sharp-edged design.

61

THE EMBARKATION OF KING HENRY VIII AT DOVER MAY XXXI MDXX.
PREPARATORY TO HIS INTERVIEW WITH THE FRENCH KING FRANCIS I

This engraving is really a reference book in itself. It answers questions about ships, from the main truck to keel, about fortifications, costumes, and cannons. It has in it, too, the stir of excitement of that May day in 1520 when King Henry the VIII of England set sail to meet Francis the First, King of France. At the place of meeting, jewels flashed, armor shone, silken banners waved; all was so richly royal that this gathering of princes and kings has been known ever since as "The Field of Cloth of Gold." The print, *Embarkation of King Henry the VIII at Dover, May 31, 1520,* was drawn by S. H. GRIMM and engraved by James Basire in 1781.

As in the engraving opposite, incredible skill must have been exercised in drawing all these small figures on copper with such clearness and accuracy. Notice how the lines vary—some light and fine for a plume or curly dog's ruff, some black and strong for the broad flank of a horse or the slanting shaft of a lance. This picture by the 17th Century French artist, JACQUES CALLOT, tells of the surrender of the Dutch town of Breda to the Spanish in the year 1625. Compared with war today, its bombs and tanks, flame-throwers and endless clanking lines of supply trucks, this *Siege of Breda* (Detail) looks like a military minuet. However, the individual soldier would have told you the battle was real enough. It must have been a field day for the dogs too—see how many you can count.

The American artist, AUDREY BULLER, has painted a very simple subject in a direct way—*Morning Glories* much at home on an old stump. The delicate tendrils, pointing to the blank corners of the background, bring the picture to a well contrived stop.

Outdoors

THE ARTIST looks at the outdoors, but he does not put on paper exactly what he sees. Outdoor objects move, light changes, leaves flutter, animals are glimpsed and then disappear. No artist can catch all this; he does not even try. Painting and drawing are a kind of translation. First of all, there is the question of taking a world where things have a front, back, and sides—three dimensions. The artist has many ways of making things seem to go back or recede into the distance, but all the time there is that stubborn sheet of paper or square of canvas which is flat when he starts and flat when he ends.

Often an artist does not even try to get distance into his picture. He makes an all-over flowered background like that in the *Unicorn Tapestry* (See "The Artist Tells A Story" chapter) , or he just puts one thing on top of another, leaving you to understand that by *top* he means *back*. The early Persian artist did this frequently. It is really a question of how near the painter wants to get to the language Nature speaks in the particular place where he happens to be. Look at van Ruysdael's *Drawing the Eel*. With his many figures and his glimpses of landscape, the artist kept as close as any painter could to what was actually before him. You can see a long way off in the distance. The third dimension is there and it makes it seem possible to walk right into that picture and join the game.

Few outdoor pictures give more sense of looking *"faraway"* than does Seurat's *Sunday on the Island of the Grande Jatte*. But much of what was in the scene Seurat left out—sticks, stones, and movement. He placed his figures so that they fit into a set design. Never do people actually arrange themselves so perfectly as this. It is the pattern, not the deep space or distance in this painting that counts.

Moon Night by William Palmer has some *"faraway"* in it too but more important is the liquid silver the moon has poured upon the fields. Nature has much to say, but the painter can rarely put more than one of her sentences into a single picture. If you had actually looked at the moonlit countryside, you would have been aware both of the distance and the light. The light being the most unusual would have fixed itself in your mind. It is this that you would have remembered and it is this chiefly that the artist paints.

Millard Sheets carries your eye over a long span in his *Landscape Near San Francisco,* but it lingers, fascinated by each step of the way, so that the journey appears to be short. You are not aware of how far you have looked. In *The*

Great Jockey, Raoul Dufy also covers a wide space, but this is more or less taken for granted. It is the motion and the excitement that comes first for him. He has caught it in every deft stroke of his brush. Distance is used here only as a kind of backdrop against which he places the winning rider.

Few pictures show more of Nature's movement than does the painting of the sea in *Black Reef* by Mattson. Waves rise with the roll of the whole ocean behind them. Water wrestles with wind which tears the waves into a white froth. It is the struggle that counts, not the space in which it takes place. In the Chinese painting, *Gentleman Playing on the Chin,* there is misty distance and perhaps more sense of space than in any of the other paintings. What seems even more important here, however, is that the artist is somehow able to put into a small bit of rock the hardness of all the rocks you have seen. He also puts into a twisted pine practically all that a whole forest could tell you. In pictures like this one, the artist does not think of Nature in relation to the language of a particular place. He has heard the one common, simple tongue she speaks wherever she is found. But even for such a painting, there was that same flat square of paper that must challenge every artist. The world is always changing, never still. You must decide how you will translate what she has to say onto your little space.

You yourself take a look outdoors. Look and look again. If you were going to paint that field, that house, that street full of children playing, what of all the things you see would you choose to put down? Would it be color, movement, restful lengths of distance and light and shadow, each crowding the other? To look at the outdoors like this is to be a painter with your mind. If you happen to like to draw, it will help you. If you don't, it will sharpen your eyes just the same, making each view of the outdoor world into a picture and every worthwhile outdoor picture into a real and well-known world.

The feeling that it is happening *now*, this minute, is in RAOUL DUFY's rapid brush lines and in his light water color wash that has the flicker of constant movement. Even the stiff, uniformed trees in the background seem alerted as if by a shared eagerness to see *The Great Jockey*.

The fairy tale words, "and it was changed into . . . ," never tell enough. How, for instance, did Cinderella's coach look as it changed, how did it look when it was half pumpkin, half transformed? In this delicate pencil *Drawing*, the contemporary American artist, PETER BLUME, has caught that magical moment not "of something was changed into . . ." but of its *being* changed.

Opposite: This is a portrait of a flower. To make such a drawing, it would seem that the artist would almost have to have been a *Columbine.* ALBRECHT DÜRER must have felt the flower's struggle to burst from the seed, the first unfolding of leaves at the touch of the sun, the moment of final blooming and, after that, the daily companionship of small butterflies and bees.

The freshness of a glittering morning is in this *Landscape Near San Francisco* by the contemporary American artist, MILLARD SHEETS. Look at it, letting your eye travel across the picture. Right in front, see how the grass, the young spirited horse and the trunks of small trees are dark. Then notice how the dead timber, the foliage of the young trees and the house are all very light. Behind them, heavy as a hill, the clump of trees is dark and the distant background alternates—now light, now shadowy. The whole is a fascinating pattern built in layers, one behind the other, like a series of screens. Each one is interesting enough to make a picture by itself.

Milch Galleries

Familiar fields and valleys grow strange on a *Moon Night*. WILLIAM PALMER, contemporary American artist, has caught a bewitched mood in the white fire of blossoming trees and in the silvered horses playing while their dull owners sleep. He has shown how rough things like wooded slopes and spiky evergreens seem rougher, and smooth things, smoother. Backs of hills and clouds and horses seem curiously alike as they give back to the moon something of the brightness she has poured upon them.

Rehn Galleries

This painting by the contemporary American artist, ALEXANDER BROOK, expresses solitude and loneliness in many ways. The little work horse, without the companionship that horses so particularly need, lingers near the abandoned house. The old engine, now but a crow's nest, long ago lost the pride it had in the days when all the country 'round came out to see it pass. Notice how the painter has given you the feeling and texture of the different kinds of rough grass growing in this *Pasture at Elk,* the unkempt coat of the horse, the rusting surface of the engine, and the cool windless covering of the sky.

Look closely at *Houses at Anvers,* and notice the different kinds of brush strokes the artist, Van Gogh, has used—curling ones for the leaves, short and rough ones for the roof, then, smooth for the plaster of the house, straight up-and-down for the wooden parts and broader, up-pushing ones for the stiff grasses in the foreground. The vines growing over the doorway and windows are like small flames, hungry to devour the old house. The edges of the stone wall, chimneys and gables are outlined with a streak of paint like the mark of a soft pencil.

With dots of paint so minute that they gave his way of working the name of Pointilism, the French painter, SEURAT, built up this perfectly planned picture of *Sunday on the Island of the Grande Jatte*. Select a small corner of it and draw the main curved lines, the bustles, parasols, the arched back of the monkey, the curled tail of the dog. Next, draw only the straight lines, the tree trunks, trouser legs, the sharp edges of the skirts or the straight backs. You will begin to see that nothing just happened in this painting. All of it was painstakingly arranged and designed.

Spring in the Country by GRANT WOOD has the charm of uncertainty. Suppose you could walk past the flowers which look as if they were made of some plastic, and over the evenly cropped woolen hills to where sheep, like penny pig banks, stand in rows, or to where distant doll-house farm buildings lie beneath neat white cotton clouds? If you became a part of this super-tidy landscape, would you be a real person or a smooth, wooden toy, forever hoeing, planting?

Drawing the Eel is a traditional Dutch game played in Winter. The players, mounted on horseback, try to catch an eel which hangs from a wire stretched across the road. There are gathered competitors and onlookers. Few paintings give such a sense of exact time and particular place as does this one by VAN RUYSDAEL, the great Dutch landscape painter of the seventeenth century. Each group within it makes a complete small picture; each adds to the feeling that you, yourself, are there and moving with the crowds. Notice how much of the painting is sky, how comparatively little is land. This is true of many outdoor pictures painted in the "Low Countries" where, so often, the earth seems but a narrow line drawn between the heavens and the sea.

With the accuracy of a map-maker or a photographer, BERNARDO BELLOTTO has preserved the Dresden of the seventeen hundreds. He has added to it, however, that which neither map nor camera ever accomplished, a quality of still crystal light, of shadows that define and outline shapes as clearly as sharp lines. He has chosen a *View of Dresden* in which the forms of square buildings, towers, and dome balance one another with absolute sureness. With vividly painted little figures, he has given a sense of life to that bright day.

Knoedler Galleries

77

A clock ticks, and that bit of time will not come again! In this delightful sketch, the Spanish artist, GOYA, has captured a moment, its gayety and sunlight, which is as fresh as the flight of *The Swing* in the wind. This moment, trapped by the quickness of a painter's brush, did not tick into the next one. After all these years, it still hangs suspended—it is now!

The Metropolitan Museum of Art

Bignou Gallery

Look at this painting for its changes from black to coolest grey; look for the lines as they become different in order to bring the river bank, bordered by small weeds, a thatched hut, tree trunk and twigs, out of the mist. Look at the part nearest to you, the part farthest away and the large space between. You will have much to see. All of a man's days, and much of the way a whole people lived and thought, went into MA YUAN's painting of *Gentleman Playing the Chin*—and so it takes a lifetime of looking.

Knoedler Galleries

COROT, painting in the French forest of Fontaineblau on a misty evening in the Spring of the year—on his favorite kind of day, hour and season, has seen it as a place to which the *Nymphs and Fauns* of ancient Greece might dare return.

Opposite: Born in Paris, PAUL GAUGUIN, wearied by dark winter skies and narrow streets of the old quarter of the city, left it and all its ties to go and live alone in the South Sea Islands. *L'Appel* was painted in the Marquesas. The artist was fascinated by the tall statue-like natives of the islands, by the strange flowers and trees that grew there. From these, he created a world of his own with such color as the people of his day had never seen before. He painted his pictures much as did the early Persians, in flat designs rather than in photographic views which lead the eye into the background of real countryside.

81

Sometimes a memory is close to a dream. You recall a day as something completely joyous, not of this world, when in reality the living of it included mosquito bites, sand in your food, and sunburn. This painting by the American artist, GEORGE BELLOWS, has in it a quality of sunny perfection which is in itself a dream. "There never was a *Picnic* quite like that one!"

The weight of water, the movement of waves as they reach the top of their roll and burst into spray, the sense of danger and of night are all in *Black Reef* by the American artist, HENRY MATTSON. Turn the painting so the sides are top and bottom and you will see, with a fresh eye, the changing path of its pattern of lights and dark.

Indoors

SHELTER, food, clothing—these are, of course, the three necessities without which mankind cannot live. The story of the way man has felt about these three things, and what he has done with them, is one of the most interesting stories in the world. Primitive man lived in caves, gnawed bones, clothed himself with leaves or skins. Then suddenly we glimpse a charming room depicted in an ancient Egyptian wall painting of some three thousand years ago. Here, food was obviously not just to be snatched at and gulped down; it was something to be looked at, something to be served on beautiful dishes decorated with flowers. Clothing was woven of fine materials and adorned with gold and jewels. Out of his three basic musts, man had created surroundings that expressed much. He had found more than the answers to the need of being housed and protected from storm and wild beasts, of being fed so that he could live from day to day, of being clothed warmly and protected from sharp stones, brambles and the whole rough surface of the earth (on which animals are safe in their soft fur coats.) He made an indoor world for himself, his family, and his friends. He called it home.

In the "Indoors" part of this book are pictures of the better times, records painted by artists throughout the years of how man has made his enlarged reflection of himself, his home. Obviously not always content to stay within the four walls of a house, man met his fellows in other places, shared amusements with them; so, in this section of the book, we also have a glimpse of places of entertainment, like the tavern or the circus. Most of the pictures, however, are of the inside of men's houses and we should therefore talk more about this aspect of "Indoors." Here we find many different ways of living changed by time, custom, climate and even more by man's feeling about himself and his fellows. Sometimes he wanted just to be grand. He therefore built a big house, furnished it richly, and clothed his family in silks and satins. This can be seen in Hogarth's *The Graham Children*. It is pleasant enough but perhaps a little over-stuffed and stiff, as if family life had been somewhat put on show or made into a parade. However, the eagerness for display is much stronger in Naiveu's *Soapbubbles*. Here the two children are all but crushed by their surroundings and by their heavy, formal clothes.

Opposite: *The French painter,* RENOIR, *has given* At the Piano *such a natural charm of gesture, such a mood of tuneful gaiety and bright enveloping warmth and sunlight that it is hard to decide what to like best about this delightful painting.*

For contrast, look at the sunny naturalness of Renoir's *At the Piano,* at the simple, ordered quiet of Chardin's *The Blessing,* or at the gaiety and "light against dark" in Jan Steen's *Twelfth Night Feast.* Vermeer, in *The Milkmaid,* has made objects of new beauty from simple things like bread, a reed basket and an earthenware jar. Here is what only a great painter can do—show rare qualities in simple things that unseeing eyes miss every day. Food, as here pictured, has become worthy of the artist's finest touch.

It is not only in the humble cottage that the artist has found harmony and grace. Again and again for kings and courts, man has had the urge to build "stately" mansions. Rarely has he glorified his ruler with more patterned elegance than in Persia. See the palace of *Young Prince Zal,* gay and jewel-like with its glittering tiled walls, intricately designed carpets, gold and silver-threaded hangings. Luxury and dignity keep company with charm in Renoir's *Madame Charpentier and Her Children,* or in the glimpse of Greek Herakles on his carved couch attended by a goddess. All of these, the artist has delighted to set down, each in his own time and after the manner of his own seeing.

But what about tomorrow? That will be your day, the day of the young. Most boys have a spell of liking to build, most girls plan clothes and later on, houses and meals. If you could bring it into being, what would tomorrow's mirror of yourself or your future home reflect? How would you make to-morrow's "Indoors" so that an artist would be eager to record it. You can little imagine how anxiously this changed world awaits all the ideas you have. Write them down or sketch them now.

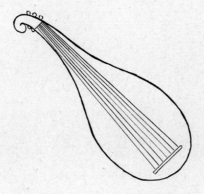

This glimpse of a small Parisian *Millinery Shop* was painted in your great-grandmother's day by the French artist, EDGAR DEGAS. The quiet little milliner, intent on a new model, is grey and wren-like among her flower-covered crowns and brims. Here is no eager, high-geared saleslady; only a calm little woman, waiting for sure and dignified custom. It is a picture not just of a hat shop, but of a restful, carefree way of living long gone by. As a design, this painting is especially delightful. Try drawing it in order to see more clearly the circles of the brims, the soft curves and planes of the young woman's head, her shoulders and the long, full dress in contrast to the straight lines of the hat stands and looped ribbons, the sharp corners of the table and the angles made by an outstretched arm and bent elbow. The deftness with which these shapes are filled into the not-quite-square frame will find its way into the movements of your pencil.

The Linen Cupboard by the Dutch artist, PIETER DE HOOCH, was painted about the time the early American Colonies were being settled. From such homes as these came the wealthiest settlers in what is now New York. The Dutch artists of this day delighted in working out the problem of how to show deep space on a flat canvas—one object, one person behind another, one room followed by a second, then a street and a house across the street seen through an open door. None have done this particular thing more skillfully than the group of seventeenth century Dutch painters to whom de Hooch belonged.

Opposite: CHARDIN's painting, *The Blessing,* is so simple that it seems to belong to any home at any time. Yet, in the perfection of the painting of each small object, from the child's drum to the little girls' quaint caps, it is peculiarly French. Even more French perhaps is its beauty of design.

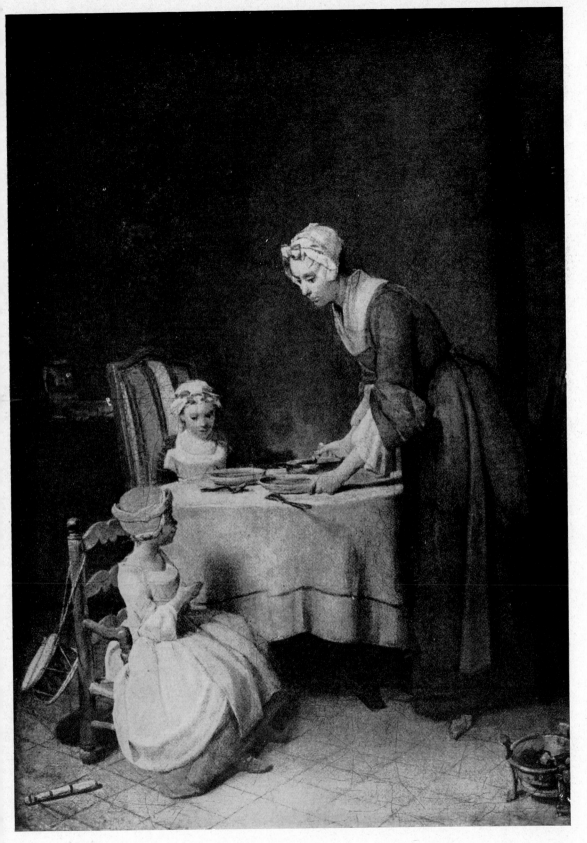

The Paris circus of the time of the painter TOULOUSE-LAUTREC, and of your great-grandfather, was small and always indoors. Clowns were often great actors whose every movement and gesture was carefully watched. In a flash, with well aimed pencil and not a line wasted, Toulouse-Lautrec draws the special and differing qualities of the cross-eyed clown, intelligent bandy-legged little horse, and alert dressed-up monkey. He also manages to give the flavor of the entire ring *At the Circus* in a day when wit and artistry, rather than bigness and noise, were demanded.

90

These children of the circus are of the same period as Toulouse-Lautrec's clown on the opposite page. RENOIR not only manages to show their rigid training in the way he poses them and in their gestures, but he also paints their persistent, childlike naturalness. Over *Two Little Circus Girls*, he has spread a bloom from his brush, sensitive to every variation of shifting light.

Art Institute of Chicago

These two Dutch children in their stiff seventeenth century costumes, with their round faces and posed and delicate hands, are almost overshadowed by the draped curtain and elaborately carved window which enclose them. Notice the heavy folds of the drapery, the full curving figures of the cupids over whose heads leafy scrolls and fruited garlands decorate an ornamental capital. Beneath them, borrowed from some ancient Roman design, more chubby cupids twist and roll about an unwilling goat. NAIVEU, who painted the two children, was seemingly less interested in them and their game of *Soapbubbles* than he was in making a picture according to the popular taste of his day.

This painting by the English artist, HOGARTH, was made at about the period George Washington was growing up in Virginia. It describes very completely the children of one of the "great houses" of England. Here in their nursery, surrounded by beautiful toys and by their pets, they have every luxury. The general air of calm and good manners is disturbed only by the cat who eyes the canary with complete "jungle" naturalness. *The Graham Children's* costume which we call "Colonial" was, of course, first that of early eighteenth century England. Proving that bravery has little to do with customs or clothes, Nicholas, the satiny infant on the left, fought his way up to the position of a high ranking officer in the Austrian service.

National Gallery, London

The Conjurer, standing alone before his counter, has just made a frog appear to have jumped from the cloak of an onlooker who is so astounded that he is quite unaware that the conjurer's helper is stealing his purse. The deceived one gapes at the trick-master as do all of those who crowd about him. They do not seem so much like several different people but like a single image of foolishness, many times repeated. BOSCH's conjurer has them all in his power. The fact that he stands alone before the dark, unbroken surface of the wall, simple and solid as a small carved figure, helps to set him apart in his malicious, yet amusing, half-black magic.

St. Germain-en-Laye, Flanders

94

Photograph: Cleveland Museum of Art

In this painting, JAN STEEN shows how *The Twelfth Night Feast,* or the feast in memory of the Three Wise Men, was observed in Holland. The youngest child, or baby, was crowned King in a celebration of shining candles and glowing fire. The star, borne by carolers, is bright in the doorway. Notice how Jan Steen uses light to tell his story—light on aprons and neckerchiefs, fiddle and hat brims; also on faces, both young and old. By means of his strong lights and darks, he keeps these many figures clear and within a single focus.

By the grace of a brush held in the deft fingers of the painter, FRAGONARD, this elegant young lady preserves a single moment scented with the expensive perfume of 18th Century France. In *The Love Letter*, the artist tells us plainly that her mood is one of pleasantly assured triumph, a feeling well known to the beauties of her day. But the little poodle, no less curled and silken than his mistress, looks out at the world with troubled eyes, as if haunted by half memories of what it is to be a dog, not just a powdered pet.

These charming little French girls, their very pretty mother, and the big watchful dog who acts as a soft couch for one of his little mistresses were painted by RENOIR. No one can paint children's blonde hair or the warm fairness of their skin more wonderfully than this nineteenth century French artist. This is a detail from the painting *Mme. Charpentier and Her Children.*

The figure of the *Milkmaid* has a naturalness like that of a tree in a forest and, at the same time, a dignity as great as that of some age-old earth goddess. She stands in perfect relation to the square that frames her and to every object within it. Eyes and spirit rest when looking at her; nothing could possibly be altered or moved. Rarely has light been painted with such skill—follow it from the window to the deepest, softest shadow and notice the changes that are made with delicate gradations. Look also at the jug of milk and the basket of bread. The Dutch artist, VERMEER, has given them the clarity and brightness of jewels.

The little *Gourmet,* which is a word defining one who likes above all else to eat, was painted by the modern Spanish-born artist, PABLO PICASSO, who has lived so long in Paris now as to seem almost French. Picasso has shown the small girl's concern with her upturned dish in many ways —by her unwavering, downward look, by the purposeful pressure of her firm, chunky body against the table, and especially by her hands, one of which determinedly covers the fullest possible length of the spoon handle, while the other holds the bowl as if it were something not only to be carefully held but to be caressed and patted.

In this early Greek vase painting of *Herakles and Athena* by an unknown artist, the hero, Herakles, rests from his earthly labors in some heavenly dwelling. Beside him stands his good friend and protectress, the Goddess Athena. His couch is richly carved, delicate food is placed before him; he is shaded by a leafy vine from which hang rich clusters of fruit. In earlier Greek vase paintings, like that of Dionysus in his ship on page 135, the figures were done in black on a soft red-brown background. They were like wonderful shadows or silhouettes. Later, artists seemed to feel the urge within themselves to do more with line, to show details, patterns in cloth, decorations on furniture or on the borders of the vase itself. In order to have their lines show more clearly, they made the figures in red on a black background. This is one of the early vases on which the new technique was used.

This wall painting, made in fresh bright colors by an unknown artist, decorated a house in the Roman city of Boscoreale (which was buried by the eruption of Mount Vesuvius some nineteen hundred and forty-five years ago). The ample Roman *Woman Playing a Harp,* who might have been mistress of the house, and the child leaning against her chair are astonishingly real, as if seen through a suddenly opened window. It is almost as though the firm solid forms had survived destruction because of the vigor with which they were painted.

The Metropolitan Museum of Art

The Chess Players by the Italian artist, FRANCESCO DI GIORGIO, might be thought of as a kind of "conversation piece" giving a glimpse of the dress of the time, as well as a popular amusement for a rainy day some five hundred years ago. Chess has not lost its fascination in all these years!

Opposite: This picture, an illustration from the Persian "Shah-Namah," or "Book of Kings," shows *Young Prince Zal* with his courtiers. Seated on his elaborate throne, he is like a central jewel in an ornate setting. Every part of this palace has its own design, and each design is enclosed within its own formal yet varied border. Truly, it has been said that Persia, and indeed all the Near East, is one of the world's great pattern boxes, so richly inventive was it in the making of designs. If you were to copy every design, count and see how many in this single painting you would have to draw.

Boys and Girls

E VERY child has said to his elders more than once, "But you don't *under-stand* me!" Often that is quite true. It is hard for grown-ups to remember how they used to feel about many things, no matter how hard they try. On the other hand, perhaps they remember some things *too* well. After all, because father liked to dig weeds, or thinks he did, it is no sign that his son wants to adopt gardening either as a hobby or a profession. An artist watching the little boy dig might have seen the reluctance in every line of his stiff, resisting body better than his own father saw it. One of the marks of an artist is a certain uncanny power which makes it possible for him to walk with another person's feet, feel with that person's hands, and see with his eyes. If the artist cannot do that he is no painter of people, at least no real portrait painter. A portrait painter would never expect Master "Airplane-Minded-Gaze-in-the-Sky" really to like digging weeds.

In the illustrations of this chapter, there are many kinds of children. Probably they puzzled their parents no end, but to the painter, each of them was in some way quite transparent. A particular child stands forth clearly for what he is; more than that, in some ways he even suggests to the artist how he is to be painted. Perhaps, that is how Vertès came to use curling brush marks for his *Girl With a Yellow Shawl*, Cranach, sharp snapping blacks and whites for his elegant duchess, and Francia, soothing, gentle lines for his wistful young duke. It also happens the other way around—when the artist chooses to paint the sort of child he understands best, the type most suited to his particular style of painting. The likeness or the feel of a person in a portrait is not just a matter of the shape of a nose or the color of eyes. It is also a matching of the quality of that person with the right kind of brush mark, a line made by the edge or tip of a pen or the smoothness or roughness in the laying on of paint.

To know even a little of what the artist knew, it is necessary to observe not only a face, a hand, a hat, a plume, but to consider how they came to appear in the exact way they do. Look at the heavy hair of Kisling's *Nancy*. It is done with the long pull of a weighted brush. Then look at the hair of Lawrence's *Pinkie*, painted swiftly with quick, windy strokes. How would Pinkie look with Nancy's deeply shadowed hair or Nancy with Pinkie's free loosely touched-in locks? Each child seems to demand her own kind of painting, or

Opposite: *To understand "arrangement of dark and light in a pattern," remember this picture by* GEORGES DE LA TOUR. *The young* Girl with a Candle, *visible only by the lighted taper, has a calm that partakes of the quietness of shadows and the safety of a light.*

(Detroit Institute of Fine Arts)

her own type of artist to paint her. Laughter and fear are not expressed in painting with the same brush stroke any more than they are in music with the same tone from a keyboard.

The painters of these young people had different purposes in mind. In some cases, they were not trying to search out a particular person, but to set forth a certain class or kind. In the East Indian miniature, *Girl with a Pet Antelope,* the unknown artist did not think of his subject as one unlike all others. He was recording, through her, all the things the court beauties had in common—their grace, their delicate hands and feet, their thick fine silks and tinkling jewels. As was so often the case in the Near East, the artist presented all this in the form of a decoration, a design.

By no means are all the European or American pictures in this part of the book portraits. As examples of some that are not, turn to de la Tour's *Girl With a Candle,* which is a study in contrasts of dark and light, a painting filled with the quietness of night after the noises and movement of day. Look also at *Young Shepherd Resting* by the French artist, Renoir. It was grace, warmth and memories of Greek myths and songs that he painted, not any living example of class or rank or of any single child for which his brush searched.

Look and see if you can discover what each of these young people meant to the artist who knew him—or her. The artist set each down as a separate person, never to be duplicated. Some are examples which typify a particular period, some portray the inner quality of a certain child, a few others are figures which stand for some idea, wide and free as youth itself.

Opposite: *In the delicate posing of* A Girl With a Pet Antelope, *in the costume, in the clear, slightly hard line, and in the feeling for decoration and design, this unknown artist is true to the traditional style of eighteenth century India.*

(Freer Gallery of Art)

In the fifteenth century, the artist, ANDREA DELLA ROBBIA, modeled this head from clay; it was then baked and glazed like pottery dishes are. This was a new way of making sculpture. It was discovered, or some say re-discovered, by Andrea's uncle, Lucca della Robbia, who in turn taught others his secret. Not only are the forms of head, shoulders, broad brows, thickly curling locks of this *Bust of the Christ Child* beautifully modeled, but the face has an expression of quiet listening—a look of eager answering that gives to the whole a persistent sense of reality and life.

In the youthful *Saint John the Baptist*, DONATELLO has modeled a head of singular purity of line. Notice the straight, delicately boned nose and the throat which is slender as a sapling. The sculptor has created a young person who can look into ordinary daily affairs and get their meaning, who can perceive how simple happenings may fit themselves into a single stirring event at a given moment in the future. This is the young seer and prophet. In every generation, his is "the voice of one crying in the wilderness."

This water color drawing of *Elisabeth of Saxony* by the 16th Century German artist, LUCAS CRANACH, THE YOUNGER, is remarkable for the way it searched out the character of the young princess. Elegant is the word for her lovely oval face, framed in the stylish fashion of her period, for her delicately shaped chin and nose and small, perfectly formed mouth. But the eyes are already cold; they look through other people, not at them with the hope of sudden friendly understanding. Responsibilities of her position have begun to weigh upon her; she is suspicious of those who try to win her favor. No longer does her mouth smile easily.

Often the best way to understand a word is to have a picture in your mind. "Style," though used so freely, is not an easy word to pin down. Sometimes a painter is able to give the quality and manner, the "style" of a person so clearly that he also sums up a whole way of living. That is what LUCAS CRANACH, THE ELDER, has done in *Anna of Denmark, Duchess of Saxony*. She has "style" to a supreme degree. If you study this and the picture opposite, the word "style" may take on added meaning.

The contemporary artist, MOÏSE KISLING, has painted not so much the way *Nancy* looks as the way she feels. He tells us she is a little girl living mostly in her own world, a world of dark fantasies. When she does notice the outside world, her feeling for it is keen, and ordinary sounds and sights echo and vibrate with strange insistence. This is the face of a sensitive, imaginative little girl.

Pinkie, painted by SIR THOMAS LAWRENCE in England in the seventeen hundreds, is as different as possible from "Nancy" (opposite). Under the curve of her bonnet and the shadow of hair, like a large, many-petalled flower, she looks out at all she sees with curious, challenging dark eyes. The eager gesture of her hand, even the flutter of her bonnet strings, is alive with her quick responses.

All the light and warmth of remembered summer days is in the nineteenth century French painting, *Young Shepherd Resting*, by RENOIR. The boy seems a part of summer, like a lusty plant that grows because of it. To feel the ease and grace of his young figure in repose, trace with your eye—or better still, with your pencil—the soft curve of extended arm and leg, the sharper but still rounded lines of bent knee and elbow.

Opposite: Earlier in his life, when he was twenty-three, the same artist, RENOIR, went for a vacation to the village of Barbizon, long a favorite spot for painters. Here he met *Mlle. Romaine Lacaux,* a little girl whose alert, wide-awake gaze he painted with an unusual balance of quiet poise and childlike dignity. Notice how the red of the flower in her lap sparkles against the cool greys and white of her dress, how they are echoed in her lips, coral earrings and, more softly, in the background where they blend with the white and greys of the misty garden pattern.

This little French boy of your great-grandfather's day was painted by Renoir with characteristic soft and broad brush strokes. The edges of "shapes" in *Portrait of Claude Painting* are blurred because the artist has painted the warm sun that shines upon them. Like a small fish seen through deep, bright waters, Claude paints with childlike intentness, shut off from all but his own work by a protecting veil of light.

Durand-Ruel

Was it the round black nose and shoe-button eyes of the dog that started this picture of a *Girl with a Yellow Shawl* going the way it went? The little black eyes, repeated in the round spangles of the shawl, give flattering intelligence and humor to the face. Perhaps, too, it was the dog's curls that sent MARCEL VERTÈS' brush ruffling along the shawl and through the child's springing locks.

Eternally gentle, *Frederigo Gonzaga,* in rich, dark velvets, touches lightly the sword by which he must later hold his own among the turbulent nobles of his time. More akin are the spring leaves and hills of the quiet Italian landscape. It is as though FRANCIA hinted at what he could not say, "this boy would be happier there keeping sheep than ever he will be ruling men."

Look closely at the face of *Edward the VI as Prince of Wales*, painted in the year 1538 by HANS HOLBEIN, THE YOUNGER. It has a charm and sweetness, stronger even than the grandeur of the princely robes or plumed and jeweled cap. For a little while, before his early death, this child held not a golden rattle but a whole nation in his pointed fingers, for he later became King of England.

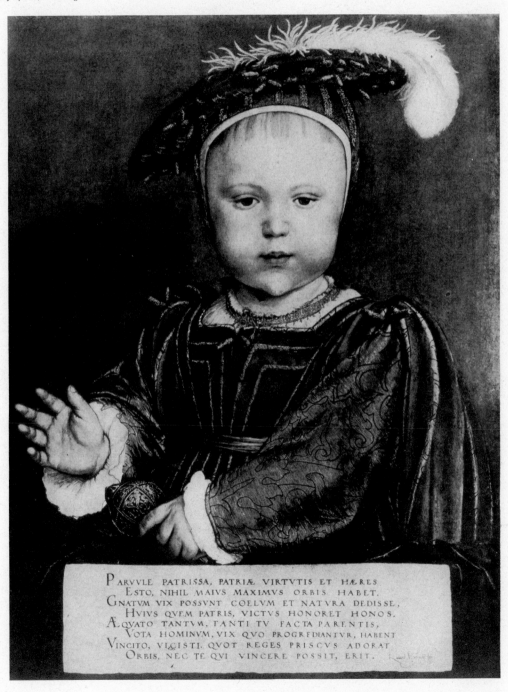

PARVVLE PATRISSA, PATRIÆ VIRTVTIS ET HÆRES
ESTO, NIHIL MAIVS MAXIMVS ORBIS HABET.
GNATVM VIX POSSVNT COELVM ET NATVRA DEDISSE,
HVIVS QVEM PATRIS, VICTVS HONORET HONOS.
ÆQVATO TANTVM, TANTI TV FACTA PARENTIS,
VOTA HOMINVM, VIX QVO PROGREDIANTVR, HABENT
VINCITO, VICISTI. QVOT REGES PRISCVS ADORAT
ORBIS, NEC TE QVI VINCERE POSSIT, ERIT.

This young *Lute Player,* firmly modeled by shadows and highlights, was drawn with crayon by the Italian artist, PIAZETTA, in the seventeen hundreds. It has a tender mood of sadness, as though, alone, the boy had met the outside world too soon. His music is not heard, it is the neglected note of the poet lost among sharp, bargaining cries of the market place.

Finely drawn, the face of this young woman, beneath hair smoothly tucked under her cap, seems the more calm and clear because of the contrast set by her richly patterned gown. Here once more an artist, POLLAJUOLO, in *Portrait of a Young Woman,* has captured the character of his model while presenting the style of a period and city—fifteenth century Florence.

Though an actual portrait of *The Ladies Amabel and Mary Jemima Yorke,* who lived in England in the seventeen hundreds, this painting by Sir Joshua Reynolds seems somehow to have been overtaken by a dream. The children, the dove, the gay little dog move in a world of haunting wistfulness and grace. The children will never grow up, but will live forever like gentle changelings in their shaded garden.

This portrait, also by SIR JOSHUA REYNOLDS, speaks of the well ordered days in the great houses of English nobility and of the elegant young creatures that grew up in these surroundings. *Lady Caroline Howard* is dressed as fashionably as her mother or her aunts. Tear a small hole in a piece of paper to make a frame for her head. See her face blocked away from party silks, satins, and laces and you will see a familiar wide-eyed look of eager childhood. The real little girl is certainly there.

Sometimes a dream becomes more real than our everyday affairs. The dragon in China was the dream of a whole people, constantly added to by poets and artists while the centuries passed. The dragon stood for power, for the nation, the Emperor, or even for life itself. CH'ÎN JUNG,

The Artist Dreams a Dream

A DREAM is really a wish, whether it's a waking dream or an "asleep" dream. Many kinds of wishes are in these pictures. One kind is called an "ideal" —the hope or wish for a perfection that does not seem a part of this world—yet! There are great ideals such as that in "Revelation," the last book in the Bible, where the writer, John, says, "And I saw a new heaven and a new earth." The English artist, William Blake, has drawn many of John's visions, none more beautiful than *The Angel of the Revelation* who is brighter than the morning. Of the many small, everyday ideals and dreams, some are wise, some foolish, some playful or quiet, some verging on "the real." Such is the Persian painting of *Youth Sleeping Under a Willow Tree*. He rests in a land almost too

in his Nine Dragons Scroll, *shows dragons as strange, mysterious beings among crags and lightning-seared clouds; yet he paints them scale by scale, feature by feature with a dreadful familiarity. The dream commands the artist.*

fair for human eyes ever to have seen, yet it is by no means completely a realm of the enchanted.

Sometimes a dream is almost all memory. It is something you recall as being more wonderful than it really was and that you hope may come again when you know it never will. Rousseau's *Medieval Castle* is that kind of half-memory, though the castle also has a "pretend" about it. Magic is certainly "wishing." What else are fairy godmothers for except to give you what you most desire? What else is the idea of the seven league boots or Hansel's and Gretel's gingerbread house?

A funny thought or fantasy has a wish in it too. You wish something out of the ordinary would happen, preferably, of course, the impossible, like suddenly sprouting unearned wings, which is the sign of grace—as Nura's angel in *Harmony* has managed to do so easily. One of the ways in which things become humorous is through unusual combinations that would never be made in actual life, as for instance, the industrious lady mouse who dutifully hangs her husband's socks to dry on her own long tail. In asleep dreams, such strange combinations appear often. You see yourself going to church in your pajamas as you try to fasten white kid gloves over your feet and struggle to hold an opened plaid umbrella.

Nature herself sometimes makes mixtures that are unusual enough to seem dreamlike. For instance, an old Ford stands abandoned on the edge of a wood. The top of the car is mostly holes and the seat is gone. Right up through the car, a young tree grows proudly. As any well brought up tree should, it wishes to feel important. It might be a little like the child who sees herself as Nura's angel, something to be admired. The tree seems to say to the car, "With all your whir and buzz, what have you come to? Trees were here before Fords." A chipmunk comes and sits on the spokeless steering wheel, flirts his tail and is off with a "cluck, chuck, I can move fast enough—if you can't." Such odd combinations are entertaining to look for and to draw.

Another way to make pictures with a dreamlike assortment of objects in them is to say four words quickly, before you have time to think—any four words: hammer, butterfly, flowerpot, mitten. Put them together just as you want. Try drawing, let us say, the hammer growing from the flowerpot, the butterfly coming out of the mitten as though it were a cocoon, the butterfly blooming in the flowerpot and the mitten grasping the hammer; the butterfly using the hammer to hit the flowerpot held by the mitten or . . . you go on. Part of the game is to arrange whatever things you choose so that they make a really good design or pattern.

Think of something you want very badly. Draw it. It will probably look more real than something you don't want but that you happen to be looking at. As for instance, you want a bicycle but you are, unfortunately, looking at an arithmetic book. Take something out of your dreams at night, good or frightening and draw it as exactly as you can. In such ways, you may work out a kind of picture that is new to you, and it also may help you to understand one by some artist that has proved puzzling. It is excellent practice. To draw dreams is very much a part of any artist's job.

Opposite: *You can't see a melody, but if you could, it would certainly only be glimpsed. This drawing entitled* Music *by* Eugene Berman *has in it the sense of being visible, just for a moment. As you look, it will disappear into the darkness as an echoing note fades into silence.*

Worcester Art Museum

The Roman god, Bacchus, known to the Greeks as Dionysus, gave to mankind the gifts of the grape and of honey. This dreamlike picture by the Italian painter, PIERO DI COSIMO, tells of the *Discovery of Honey,* not by sober farming folk but by satyrs. These half-man, half-goat creatures were the followers of Bacchus and friends of Pan, God of Forest and Pasture. A grown-up satyr beats on a copper pot to make a loud noise that will cause the bees to swarm in the hollow tree from which honey can later be gathered. Beside him, a likeness in miniature, sits a baby satyr with tiny hoofs and long pointed ears, a strange blend of the human and animal.

Opposite: To be ever searching for impossible melodies on a stringless harp is indeed to know the words "empty as a dream." With his twisting lines and smudges of water color wash, EUGENE BERMAN in *Fantasy* has managed to draw that bewitched weariness of having to go on senselessly trying to do what no one ever can, a feeling that is so often a part of dreams.

(Julien Levy Gallery)

The early American artist, RYDER, paints Shakespeare's *Forest of Arden* at the moment when Rosalind and Celia are lost in the darkened wood. A tree lifts broken fingers to the sky; shadows lurk with secrets hidden in their cloaks. A story, as full of changing mood and scene as this one, says to every artist, "Dream me, *As You Like It.*"

The French artist, HENRI ROUSSEAU, painted this enchanted *Medieval Castle* as though it were made of black velvet, the houses and sky of moonlit white satin. Try drawing the curves of the towers, the trees, the pointed shapes of the roofs and hills. You will have a delightfully simple design.

Orpheus, ancient Greek spirit of music, charmed man and beast. The ringing tones of his harp sound down the centuries. Each age has heard them, and each has pictured Orpheus in its own way. In fifteenth century Italy, CIMA DA CONEGLIANO shows Orpheus playing not on a lyre or harp, but on a viol such as the troubadours of his own day used. It is true the artist gave Orpheus a draped cloak and a tunic faintly suggesting Greek armor—but, in reality, here is Orpheus reborn as a young Italian lad whom Cima da Conegliano might have seen on most any morning singing to the spring.

These *Animal Studies* by an unknown Venetian artist of the LOMBARD SCHOOL (15th Century) show quite a different treatment from those in the picture opposite. Here the artist is beginning to work them into delicate, fanciful and stylized designs, perhaps to be used on tooled leather or the painted margin of a book.

Fogg Museum of Art

Munich

EXEKIAS, a vase painter in Greece more than twenty-four hundred years ago, tells of the voyages of *Dionysus in his Ship*. The God of Wine and Pleasure, crowned with ivy, and with a great drinking horn in his hand, rests at ease in his ship with its swelling sail. That it is a warship is clear from the ramming device at the prow. On either side of the mast, twin vines grow up, richly laden with ripe fruit. Often Dionysus was imagined as he is pictured here, faring far to bring precious gifts, like that of the grape, to man.

Opposite: In this Persian painting, the unknown artist dreams a dream of one who, himself, dreams beneath a willow tree. The artist's dream is one of vermilion and gold, violet and moss green, touched with deeper purple in iris and pointed slippers, with black in the surprised round eyes of small flowers fringed with white. He dreams of softly curving forms in the slender, dripping branches of the tree and in the relaxed body of the sleeper. As to the *Youth Sleeping Under a Willow* Tree, himself, what he dreams can only be guessed, but it is Spring.

(Cleveland Museum of Art)

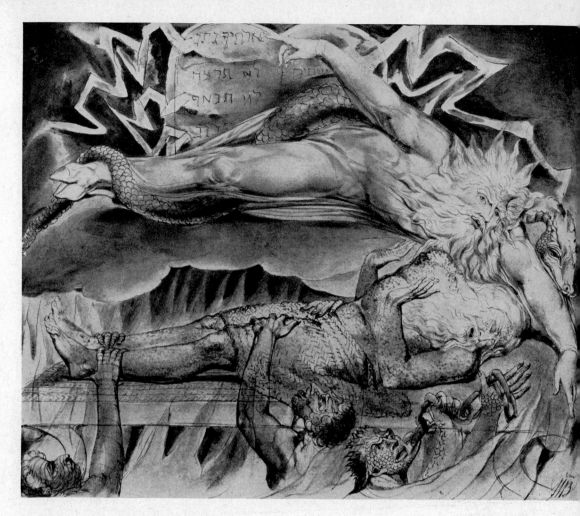

According to the story in the Bible, the Lord tested the faith of his servant, Job, by sorely afflicting him. With unforgettable power and mastery of line, the English artist, WILLIAM BLAKE, has drawn the agony of *Job's Evil Dreams*. "Then thou scarest me with dreams, and terrifiest me through visions, so that my soul chooseth strangling, and death rather than my life."

Opposite: In this picture, *Angel of the Revelation,* WILLIAM BLAKE shows the small figure of John writing Revelation, the last book in the Bible. There appeared before John a "strong angel coming down out of heaven, arrayed in a cloud; and the rainbow was upon his head, and his face was the sun, and his feet as pillars of fire; and he had in his hand a little book open: and he set his right foot upon the sea and his left foot upon the earth."

In a central panel with two flanking panels or wings, HIERONYMUS BOSCH, early Flemish artist, painted with great detail the story of the *Temptation of Saint Anthony.* This holy man led so pure a life that he aroused the fury of Satan who sent demons to tempt the good man; lions, tigers, scorpions, and nameless horrors were summoned to torture him. After years of suffering, Anthony triumphed over all of these and became one of the great saints of the church. In this very small part of the left panel of the picture, Hieronymus Bosch has placed some of the strange dreamlike figures which were continually thronging his own mind and appearing from the tip of his brush as if by magic—often a black and witch-like magic. This fascinating artist is one of the greatest dreamers of strange dreams and unearthly fantasy to be found in all the long list of painters, old or new.

Opposite: With a May tree for a mast, *The Ship of Fools,* by HIERONYMUS BOSCH, is a strange ship. In it, seemingly, are people who care not where they go, so go not anywhere. The pilot leaves his post to dine. Sailors pluck fruit from near-by bushes or swim in the sea as they fish or play and sing a rowdy song.

HIERONYMUS BOSCH, has made the Garden of Eden into a kind of dream garden where the real and unreal meet. Here, in a detail of *The Garden of Delight,* he has placed animals both actual and imaginary. The garden fountain, a kind of center pedestal, is designed with exactness. Behind it, as if on the edges of a nightmare, figures become less clear, plants seem half fish, trees grow from stone mill wheels and birds nest in houses meant only for trolls or dwarfs.

WILLIAM BLAKE's drawing, *Comus Addressing the Lady,* is an illustration for the poem "Comus," written by John Milton in 1634. Comus, the son of the enchantress Circe, himself a weaver of mighty spells, hides under the disguise of a shepherd and meets the Lady in a wood. The Lady fears some grave misadventure because she does not know of or see the winged protection of the Spirit, "swift as the sparkle of a glancing star." It is hard to say just how Blake takes the beholder to an enchanted place. Perhaps it is the airy lightness of the Spirit, the pale delicacy of the Lady, or in the sleek panther-like power of Comus who stalks her, his shepherd's cap in one hand and his "charming rod" hidden behind his back. Perhaps it is a sense of waiting stillness given by the many up-and-down lines, like those of a vaulted cathedral. More probably, it is the fact that Blake, a poet and dreamer of great dreams, knew the world of magic better than this everyday world of pudding and pence.

Museum of Fine Arts, Boston

Nura's picture, *Harmony,* is perhaps a very little child's dream of herself after she has helped wash dishes and made the beds—and nobody except herself realizes how good she is. But *she* knows! She is an angel with suns in her crown, with wings, a mandolin on her knee and three little birds to help with the tune. It is what was meant by a little boy who, after being very unselfish and not being thanked enough, said, "What I really ought to have is one of those lights around my head!"

SALVADOR DALI is one of those modern artists who is said to paint the objects of the outside world only as they help him put down his own dreams. The form of the bell ringing in the tower, repeated in the girl jumping rope, also the bright sun and ink-spilled shadows are long-ago childhood thoughts to which the artist-dreamer at the door can never quite return. Or perhaps *Nostalgic Echo* is all something else. What do *you* think?

The city with tall buildings, church steeple, small crowded factories or apartment houses is modern. The dream of the winged rider and the black horse is old as the cloudy sky through which they move. "Spirit of night! Wrap thy form in a mantle gray, star-inwrought! Bind thine hair with the eyes of day."* Yet the forms in this picture are new in certain ways—thin, sharp, a little brittle. Perhaps it is because dreamers today do not quite believe in their dreams as the ancients did. The dreams of old-time seemed so real they were often made into solid figures of stone and clay that stood upon the earth like giants. RAYMOND BREININ, contemporary American, has painted the background of *The Night* with special skill. For a sky, he has created a tissue of light and shadow; mists change and breathe and move across it.

* from Shelley.